OWEN DAVEY

SMART ABOUT
SHARKS

FLYING EYE BOOKS

London | Los Angeles

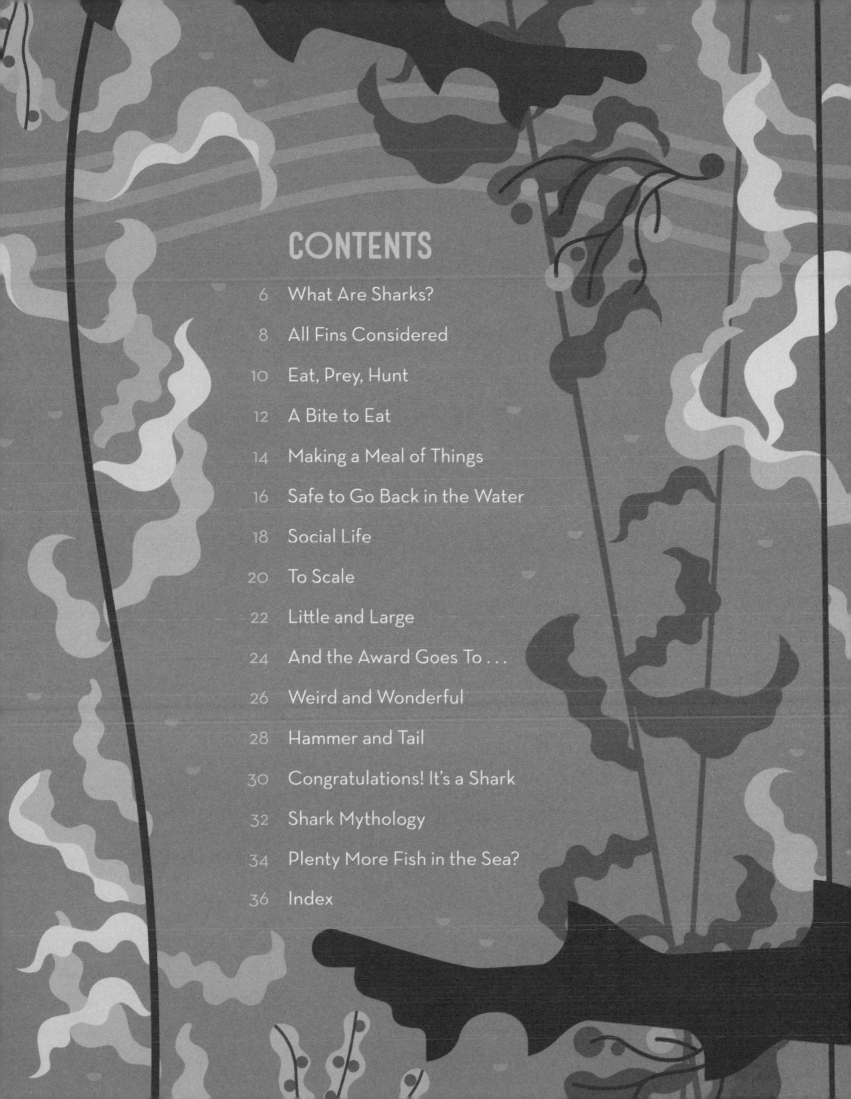

CONTENTS

WHAT ARE SHARKS?

Sharks are a group of fish that don't have any bones in their bodies. Their skeletons are cartilage, which is what the tips of our nose and ears are made of.

Home Sweet Home

Sharks are found in nearly every ocean on the planet. The type of place where an animal lives is called a **habitat**. Shark habitats range from the bustling coral reefs to the vast open oceans.

Silky sharks from above

Nom Nom

All sharks are **carnivores**, which means they only eat meat. They aren't too picky either, eating fish, seals, dolphins, turtles, crabs, squid, sea birds, and tiny sea creatures called zooplankton.

The varied diet of sharks

Uncharted Waters

It is only through new technology that we can properly begin to study the oceans and the wonderful creatures that live there. We still have a lot to learn and discover.

But for now, let's don our wetsuits, race to the water's edge, and dive beneath the surface. Get ready to explore the exciting world of some of the most successful underwater hunters on Earth, and become *Smart About Sharks!*

ALL FINS CONSIDERED

Sharks evolved over 420 million years ago. That makes them more than 200 million years older than dinosaurs! Humankind has only been roaming the Earth for less than 3 million years. These perfect predators were here long before us and have survived several mass extinctions.

There are now over 500 unique shark species alive today. Each of these species has become specially adapted in a process known as **evolution**. Evolution is the process by which animals have changed over time. Certain characteristics are passed down from generation to generation that help them survive.

These surviving sharks are split into eight groups (known as **orders**) depending on specific criteria.

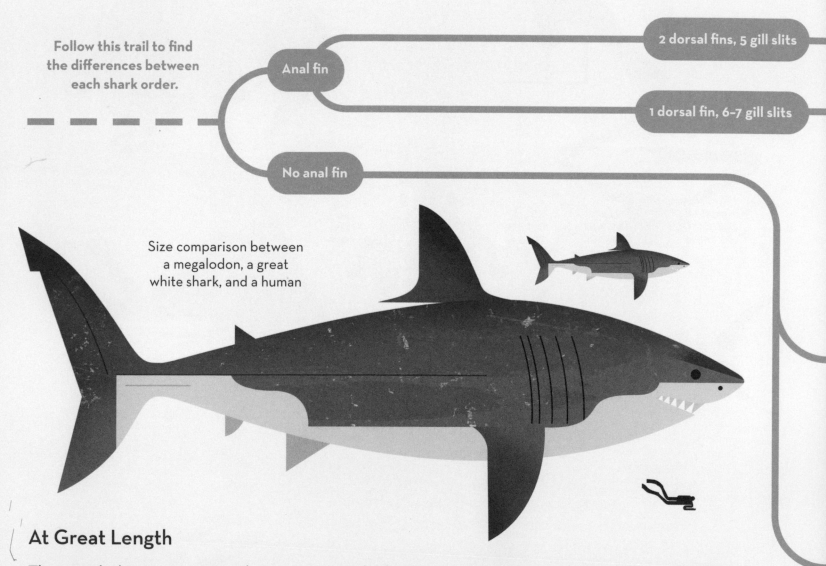

Follow this trail to find the differences between each shark order.

Anal fin

2 dorsal fins, 5 gill slits

1 dorsal fin, 6–7 gill slits

No anal fin

Size comparison between a megalodon, a great white shark, and a human

At Great Length

The megalodon is now extinct but it was once the largest shark to have lived. This massive prehistoric predator was thought to be a whopping 50 to 60 feet long and could have weighed the same as 30 great white sharks. These estimates are based on the size of fossilized megalodon teeth, which grew to 7 inches long: that's almost the size of a human's head!

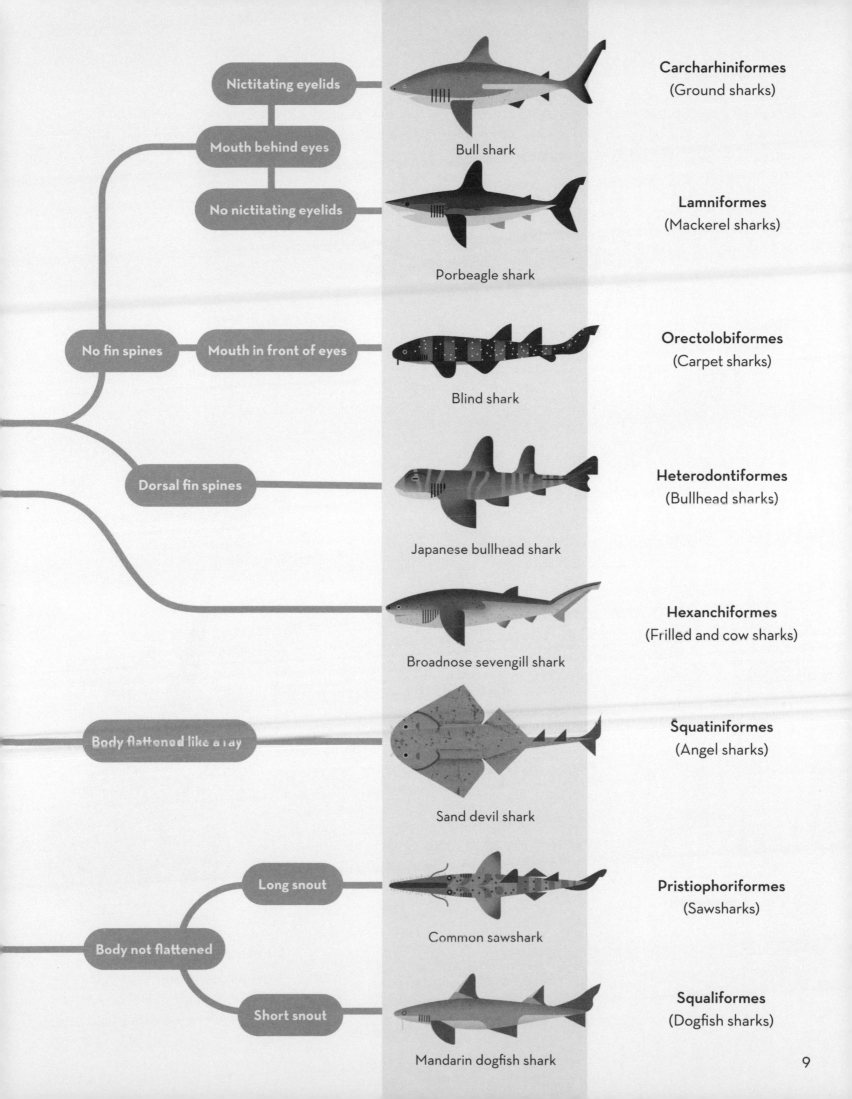

Nictitating eyelids

Mouth behind eyes

No nictitating eyelids

No fin spines

Mouth in front of eyes

Dorsal fin spines

Body flattened like a ray

Long snout

Body not flattened

Short snout

Carcharhiniformes
(Ground sharks)

Bull shark

Lamniformes
(Mackerel sharks)

Porbeagle shark

Orectolobiformes
(Carpet sharks)

Blind shark

Heterodontiformes
(Bullhead sharks)

Japanese bullhead shark

Hexanchiformes
(Frilled and cow sharks)

Broadnose sevengill shark

Squatiniformes
(Angel sharks)

Sand devil shark

Pristiophoriformes
(Sawsharks)

Common sawshark

Squaliformes
(Dogfish sharks)

Mandarin dogfish shark

9

EAT, PREY, HUNT

Sharks are some of the most successful predators in the animal kingdom. They have evolved with several remarkable super powers to help them hunt prey. Take a closer look at this Caribbean reef shark to discover the secrets behind their success.

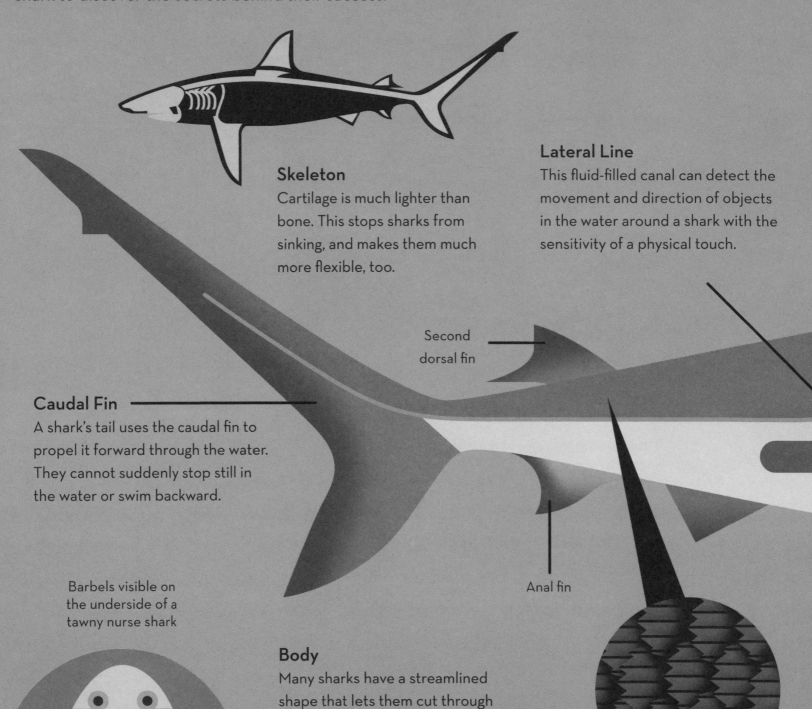

Skeleton
Cartilage is much lighter than bone. This stops sharks from sinking, and makes them much more flexible, too.

Lateral Line
This fluid-filled canal can detect the movement and direction of objects in the water around a shark with the sensitivity of a physical touch.

Second dorsal fin

Caudal Fin
A shark's tail uses the caudal fin to propel it forward through the water. They cannot suddenly stop still in the water or swim backward.

Barbels visible on the underside of a tawny nurse shark

Anal fin

Body
Many sharks have a streamlined shape that lets them cut through the water quickly, quietly, and with great speed.

Barbels
Some sharks have these strange fleshy moustaches that help them detect prey.

Denticles
Shark skin is covered in tiny teeth called denticles, which feel rough to the touch. This helps reduce friction in the water, so the shark can swim faster.

Spines

Some species of shark have spines in their dorsal fins. These spines are used as protection from predators and can excrete poison.

Dorsal Fin

This infamous fin is used for stabilizing the movement of the shark as it swims.

Eyes

Sharks have excellent eyesight. They are thought to be up to ten times better at seeing underwater than we are.

Ears

Shark hearing is exceptional, despite their ears being inside their body. Some sharks can hear struggling prey from more than two football fields away.

Nares

Shark nostrils are known as **nares**. Some species of shark are thought to be able to smell one drop of blood dissolved within one million drops of seawater.

Pectoral Fins

These create lift for a shark, like wings do on an airplane. They help keep the shark afloat.

Mouth

Filled with teeth

Gills

Fish can only breathe when water passes over the slits in the sides of their heads called gills.

Ampullae of Lorenzini

These freckle-like dots on a shark's nose can detect electrical currents from living animals, even if they are buried under sand.

A BITE TO EAT

Unlike most other animals, shark jaws aren't firmly attached to the rest of their skull so they can push their jaws forward as they bite, giving them that extra bit of reach. Sharks don't chew their food—they can't! Instead, they either swallow their prey whole, crush it, or bite off chunks of flesh.

The average shark has 40 to 45 teeth and they have rows and rows of backup teeth for when the front tooth is broken off. Throughout the life of a shark, they may go through 30,000 teeth!

1 Sand tiger shark tooth   **2** Bull shark tooth   **3** Broadnose sevengill shark tooth   **4** Port Jackson shark jaws   **5** Great white shark tooth   **6** Great white shark jaws   **7** Frilled shark teeth   **8** Great hammerhead shark tooth   **9** Cookiecutter shark jaws   **10** Tiger shark tooth   **11** Basking shark teeth   **12** Lemon shark tooth   **13** Shortfin mako shark tooth

Something to Sink Your Teeth Into

Great white shark teeth are 2 inches long and triangle shaped. They have a serrated edge with dozens of tiny razor-sharp points on them, which can even cut through tough skin, muscle, and bone.

Despite being the second largest fish in the ocean, the basking shark eats some of the smallest creatures, called zooplankton, by sifting them from the water using bristlelike parts on its gills known as **gill rakers**.

Basking shark

Sand tiger sharks have narrow needlelike teeth used to pierce and trap slippery prey like fish, rays, and squid.

Port Jackson sharks have pointed teeth at the front of their mouths, but flatter teeth at the back, similar to human molars. These molarlike teeth are used for crushing prey with hard shells, just like a nut cracker.

Spotted eagle ray

Port Jackson shark
with an oyster

MAKING A MEAL OF THINGS

Finding food is only part of the trouble—catching prey can be a very difficult task. When sharks sense an opportunity to attack, they can use a number of ways in order to bag themselves a meal.

Strength in Numbers

Blacktip sharks have been seen herding large groups of fish known as a **school** or a **shoal.** Some blacktip sharks will swim underneath while the others swim in a circle around them, cutting off their escape from all angles. The dense pack of fish created is called a **bait ball**. Each shark will then take turns attacking the bait ball until nothing but a shower of fish scales is left.

Cut and Run

Cookiecutter sharks latch onto their prey with suction created by their fleshy mouth and tongue. Biting into the larger animal with its teeth, it then twists its body around and cuts a circular chunk of flesh from the creature. Scars from cookiecutter shark attacks are seen on everything from whales to great white sharks.

Hide-and-Seek

Sand tiger sharks are the only known species of shark to gulp in air and store it in their stomachs. This allows them to float above the ocean floor without moving or making a sound. Their prey don't have a clue what's coming until it's too late.

Sand tiger shark

Cookiecutter shark

Now You See Me, Now You Don't

Camouflage can be very important when hunting. Many sharks are a dark color on top, and a light color below—this is called **countershading**.

Tasselled wobbegong shark

The wonderfully named tasselled wobbegong shark has taken camouflage to the extreme. It perfectly blends into the sea floor as it is covered in small tassels that look like pieces of coral. It is so well hidden that it simply lies still and waits for its unsuspecting prey.

SAFE TO GO BACK IN THE WATER

Featured Creatures: Great white shark, Lamniformes

The rock star of the shark world has to be the great white shark. They are fast, powerful, and excellent hunters. Great white sharks are highly intelligent with individual personalities and a strong sense of curiosity.

Bite Me

With an exaggerated reputation for being man-eaters, great white sharks have dominated TV and movies for decades. But shark attacks are extremely rare. Great white sharks are not thought to actively hunt humans, and most attacks are on surfers. From below, the silhouette of a surfer is very similar to that of a seal or a sea turtle. Great white sharks are also thought to use "test bites" to determine whether something is worth eating.

Brown fur seal

Green sea turtle

Human on a surfboard

The Hunter Becomes the Hunted

The great white shark is an **apex predator**. This means that there are very few predators that hunt it. The only real threat to a great white are orcas, known as killer whales. These huge members of the dolphin family can flip the sharks onto their backs and hold them in place until they suffocate.

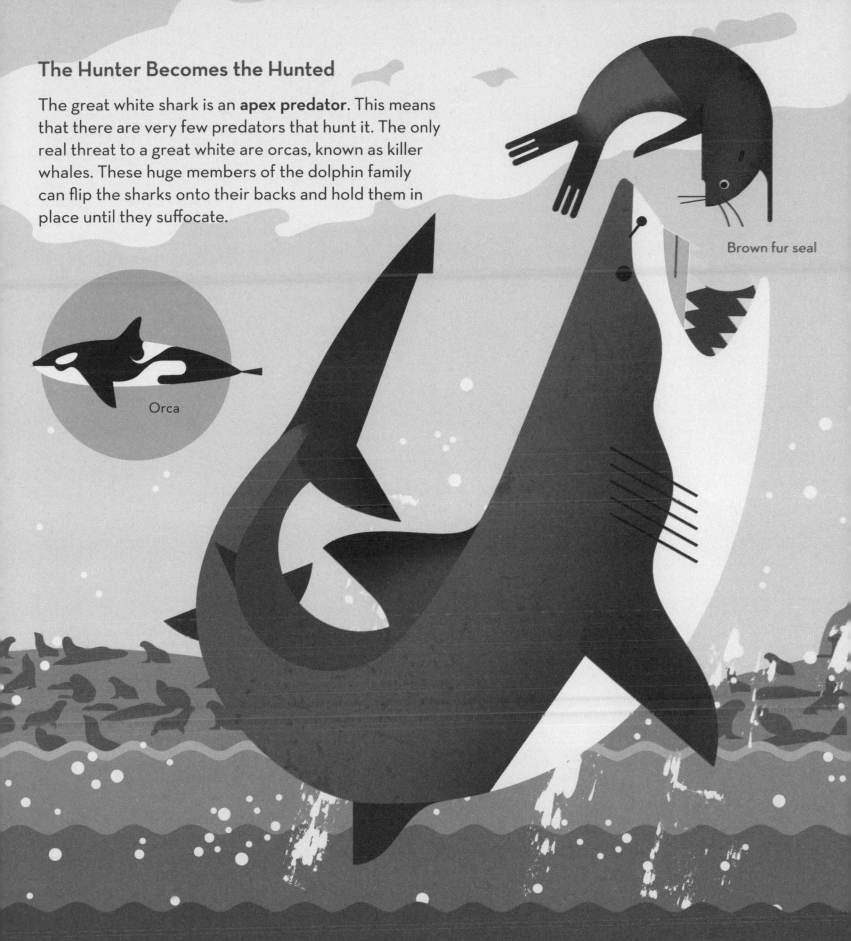

Orca

Brown fur seal

Surprise, Surprise

Seals can easily outsmart a shark if they see it coming, so great white sharks stage surprise attacks. Stalking the seals until the perfect moment, the shark will attack from below. Using only a few massive swipes of their tail, a great white shark can snatch the seal from the surface and leap up to ten feet out of the water, landing with the prize firmly in its jaws.

SOCIAL LIFE

Sharks have a reputation for being solitary creatures, but this is not always the case. Sharks of all sorts come together for protection, to feed, or to mate and make more sharks.

Feeding Frenzy

When there is a big school of fish or a large animal dies, everyone wants a taste. Large whale carcasses can draw up to 40 great white sharks. When many sharks come together to feed, it is known as a **feeding frenzy**. Great white sharks will sometimes compare sizes to determine who gets first dibs on a kill.

Great white sharks swim side by side to measure their length

Great white shark displays length to a competitor

Great white sharks splash the water with their tails — the bigger splash wins.

A school of spurdog sharks

Back to School

Some sharks are very social, spending their time in groups or schools made up of thousands of individuals. In the case of the spurdog shark, large groups could mean protection from other predators or help with hunting.

Clean Up

Remoras and pilot fish keep close to sharks, such as the grey reef shark, eating leftovers and parasites that feed off the shark. This keeps the shark healthy and protects the remora and pilot from other predators. When both parties benefit from an alliance, it is known as a **symbiotic** relationship.

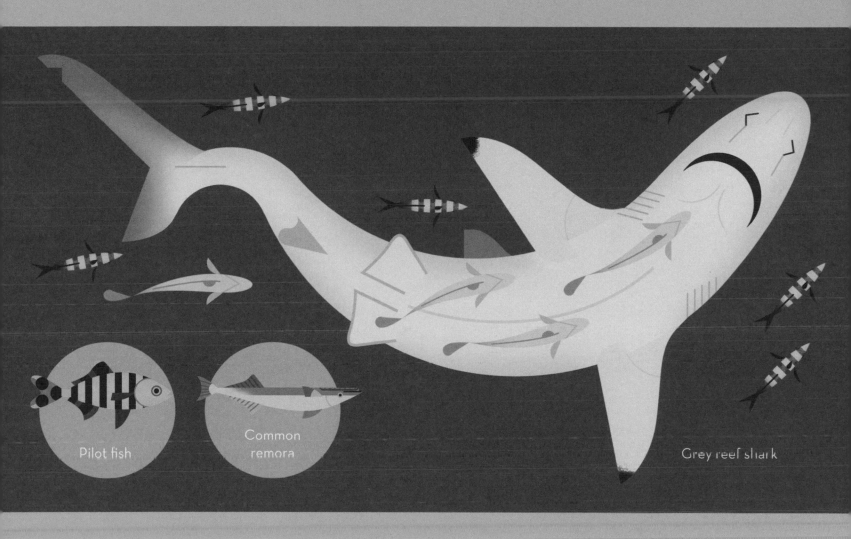

Pilot fish

Common remora

Grey reef shark

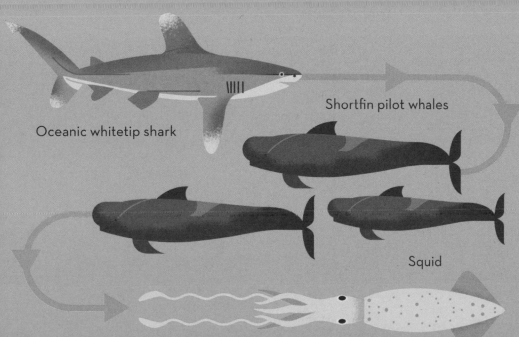

Oceanic whitetip shark

Shortfin pilot whales

Squid

Follow the Crowd

Oceanic whitetip sharks are commonly seen following large groups of shortfin pilot whales as they dive down into the depths. They are not hunting the pilot whales, but are instead thought to have learned that these pods of whales are very good at finding squid; by hanging around with them, it helps them find a meal.

TO SCALE

Different sharks don't tend to hang around in groups quite this close! Here you can see the average size of different species of shark compared to humans and each other.

Cookiecutter shark

Blind shark

Sand tiger shark

Dwarf lanternshark

Spurdog shark

Common sawshark

Basking shark

Caribbean reef shark

Broadnose sevengill shark

3 feet

Porbeagle shark

Bull shark

Mandarin dogfish shark

Scalloped hammerhead shark

Whale shark

Swell shark

Oceanic whitetip shark

Great white shark

Sand devil shark

Banded shark

Japanese bullhead shark

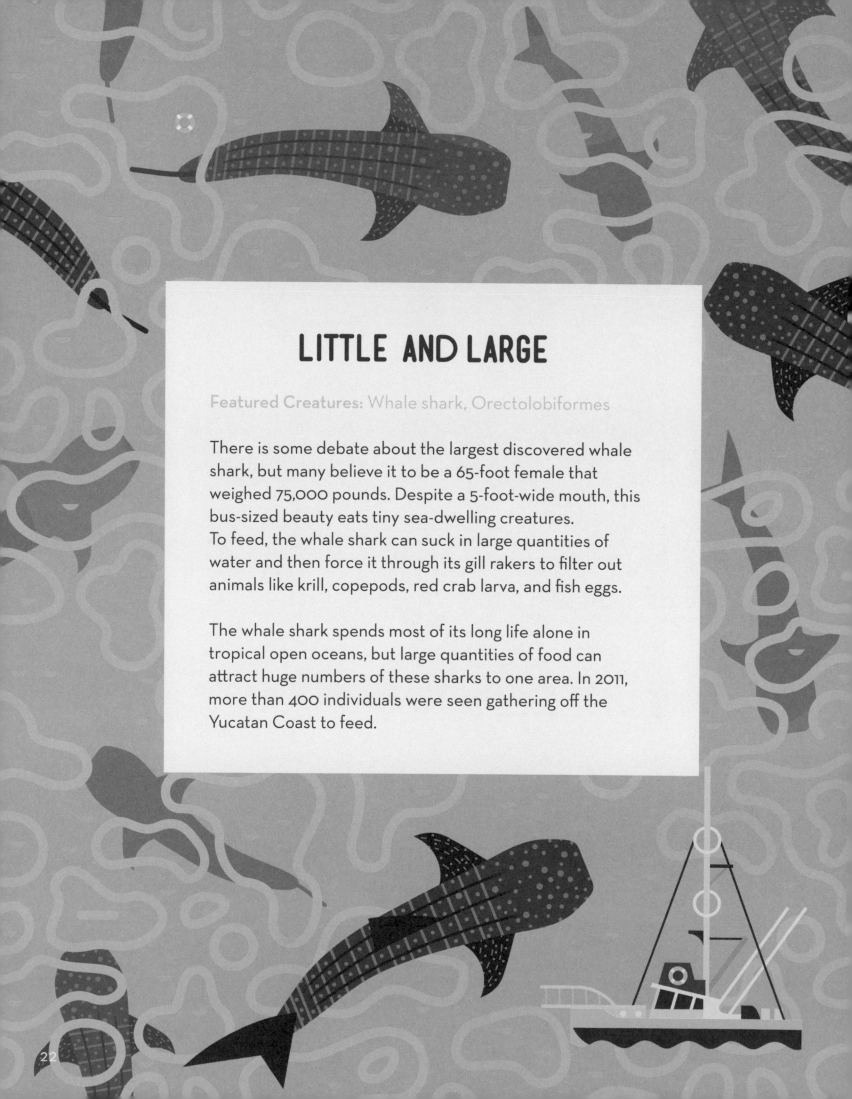

LITTLE AND LARGE

Featured Creatures: Whale shark, Orectolobiformes

There is some debate about the largest discovered whale shark, but many believe it to be a 65-foot female that weighed 75,000 pounds. Despite a 5-foot-wide mouth, this bus-sized beauty eats tiny sea-dwelling creatures.
To feed, the whale shark can suck in large quantities of water and then force it through its gill rakers to filter out animals like krill, copepods, red crab larva, and fish eggs.

The whale shark spends most of its long life alone in tropical open oceans, but large quantities of food can attract huge numbers of these sharks to one area. In 2011, more than 400 individuals were seen gathering off the Yucatan Coast to feed.

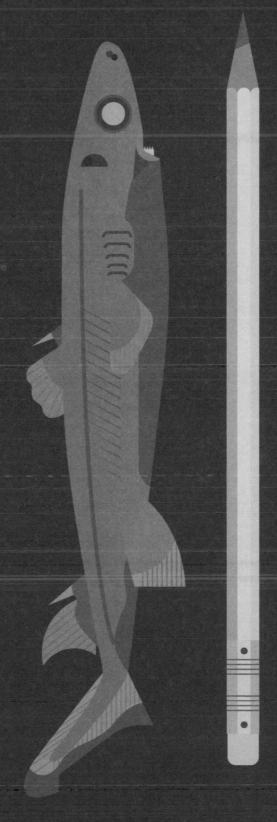

Featured Creatures:
Dwarf lanternshark, Squaliformes

Like humans, sharks start out small and get bigger as they get older. This makes it difficult to tell exactly which is the smallest shark, because a small shark may not be fully grown.

There are, however, a few strong contenders for the world's smallest shark, all of which could fit in the palm of an adult's hand. The dwarf lanternshark is widely considered the smallest, reaching a maximum of just over 8 inches (about the size of a standard pencil).

Living deep in the oceans, these guys can produce their own light, which is thought to camouflage them, attract mates, lure in prey, or act as a way of communication. Around a tenth of all shark species can produce light.

A life-size illustration of a dwarf lanternshark next to a pencil.

AND THE AWARD GOES TO...

The shortfin mako shark bags the prize for being the fastest. It is hard to measure the exact speed of this underwater sprinter, but estimates suggest it can swim 40 miles per hour or faster.

This incredible shark also wins another award, for the highest jump. When directed toward the surface, their extraordinary speed can transfer into spectacular somersault leaps of up to 20 feet out of the water.

The epaulette shark has developed the astounding ability of walking out of water. When hunting prey in rock pools, the epaulette shark can hold its breath for 60 times longer than a human and uses its strong fins to shuffle over the rocks back to the sea.

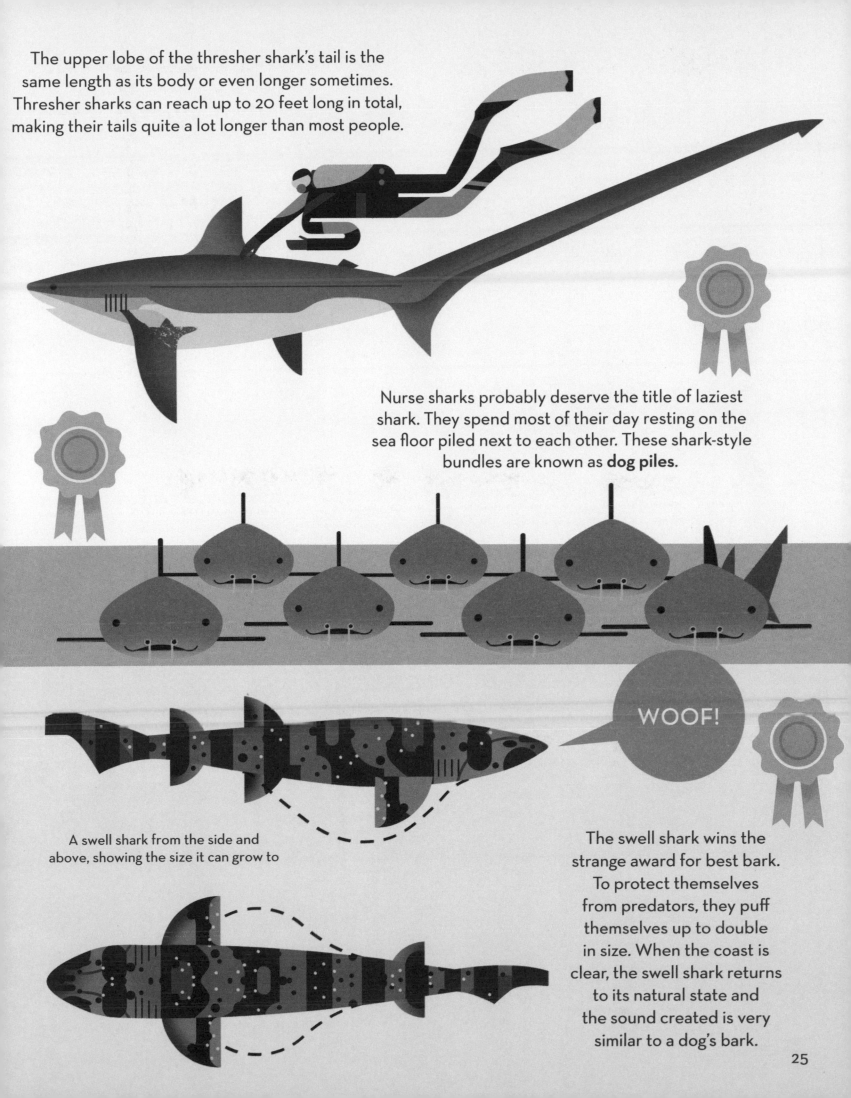

The upper lobe of the thresher shark's tail is the same length as its body or even longer sometimes. Thresher sharks can reach up to 20 feet long in total, making their tails quite a lot longer than most people.

Nurse sharks probably deserve the title of laziest shark. They spend most of their day resting on the sea floor piled next to each other. These shark-style bundles are known as **dog piles**.

A swell shark from the side and above, showing the size it can grow to

The swell shark wins the strange award for best bark. To protect themselves from predators, they puff themselves up to double in size. When the coast is clear, the swell shark returns to its natural state and the sound created is very similar to a dog's bark.

WEIRD AND WONDERFUL

Ornate Angel Shark
Like all angel sharks, these unusual looking fish have winglike fins and eyes on the tops of their heads.

Tropical Sawshark
These fearsome fish use their long snout (known as a **rostrum**) to attack both predator and prey.

Goblin Shark
With a face this bizarre looking, it's lucky they live in the darkness of the deep sea.

Birdbeak Dogfish Shark
So called after their oddly long and flat snout.

Horn Shark
Preferring to take shelter during the day, these sharks hunt at night.

Frilled Shark
You might mistake these sharks for a giant eel. Their jaws can open very wide to take in large prey.

Megamouth Shark
An extremely rare species of filter-feeder, with strange mouths that glow in the dark.

Pyjama Shark
These striped sharks have markings very reminiscent of zebras.

HAMMER AND TAIL

Featured Creatures: Scalloped hammerhead shark, *Sphyrnidae*

Hammerhead sharks are easily recognizable by their strange hammer-shaped heads, which are known as a **cephalofoil**.

Scallop shell

The scalloped hammerhead shark is the most commonly found species of hammerhead, and is distinct from the others by the bumpy shape on its snout that looks like a scallop shell.

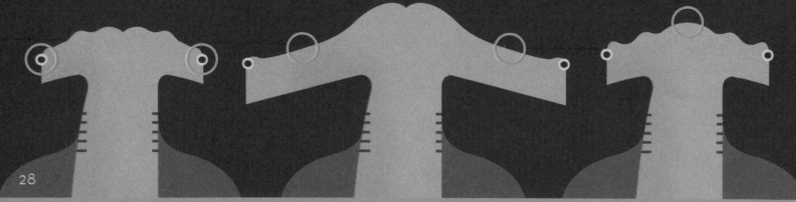

Unlike the scalloped hammerhead shark, the great hammerhead shark doesn't have the little nodules at either end of its head.

The winghead shark has a longer cephalofoil than the scalloped hammerhead shark.

The smooth hammerhead shark lives up to its name and has a smooth tip to its snout.

Super Sight

The hammerhead shark's cephalofoil works a bit like a metal detector, scanning the ocean floor. With eyes on either end of their head, the scalloped hammerhead shark has a better field of vision than other sharks, especially when moving its head from side to side. It has only two blind spots, which are just in front of its snout and right behind its head. The diagrams below show the fields of vision of humans and a few sharks, from above.

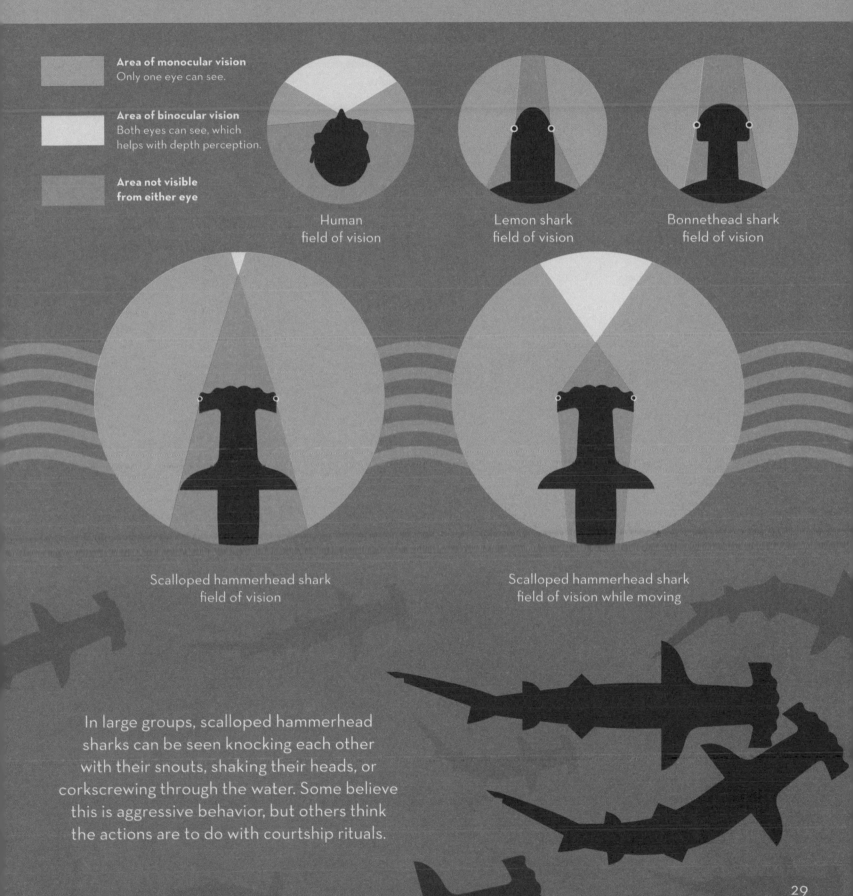

Area of monocular vision
Only one eye can see.

Area of binocular vision
Both eyes can see, which helps with depth perception.

Area not visible
from either eye

Human
field of vision

Lemon shark
field of vision

Bonnethead shark
field of vision

Scalloped hammerhead shark
field of vision

Scalloped hammerhead shark
field of vision while moving

In large groups, scalloped hammerhead sharks can be seen knocking each other with their snouts, shaking their heads, or corkscrewing through the water. Some believe this is aggressive behavior, but others think the actions are to do with courtship rituals.

CONGRATULATIONS! IT'S A SHARK

For any species to survive it must reproduce to create new generations. This means that they need to make babies, which in the shark world are called **pups**. Litters can range from only a few pups for species like the great white shark, to more than 100 pups for creatures like the blue shark.

Great white
shark pups

Blue shark pups

Uterus (Viviparity)

Some sharks give birth to live young. The pups develop inside an area of the shark called a **uterus** before they enter the world. During this time, they get all their needs directly from their mother. This process can take anywhere from a few months to over two years, depending on the species.

Eggs (Oviparity)

Some sharks lay eggs into well-hidden areas in the ocean. These eggs are protected by a thick leathery outer casing, often called a **mermaid's purse**, which makes it harder for predators to get at the pup inside. The pup will feed off an energy-rich yolk sac within the egg, until it is ready to enter the ocean.

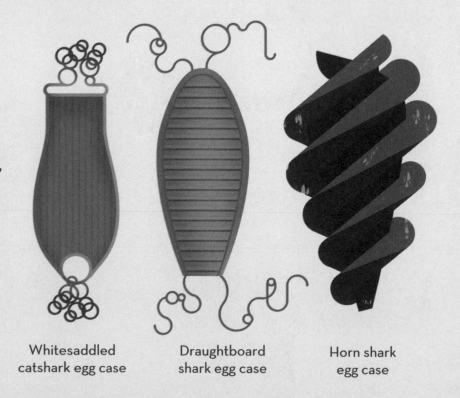

Whitesaddled
catshark egg case

Draughtboard
shark egg case

Horn shark
egg case

Uterus & Eggs (Ovoviviparity)

Many shark species grow in eggs within their mother, feeding off the yolk sac before emerging into the uterus. Some species of shark pups, like the sand tiger shark, will even hunt down their brothers and sisters and eat them too!

A sand tiger shark with two uterus lobes filled with eggs and two competing pups

Do it Alone

Sharks don't make the most caring parents, usually swimming away without a second thought for their pups. Luckily the pups are actually tiny fully formed predators, ready to hunt their own food. Some pups look like miniature versions of their mothers, while other species like the zebra shark are born with extra camouflage that might help them hide from predators.

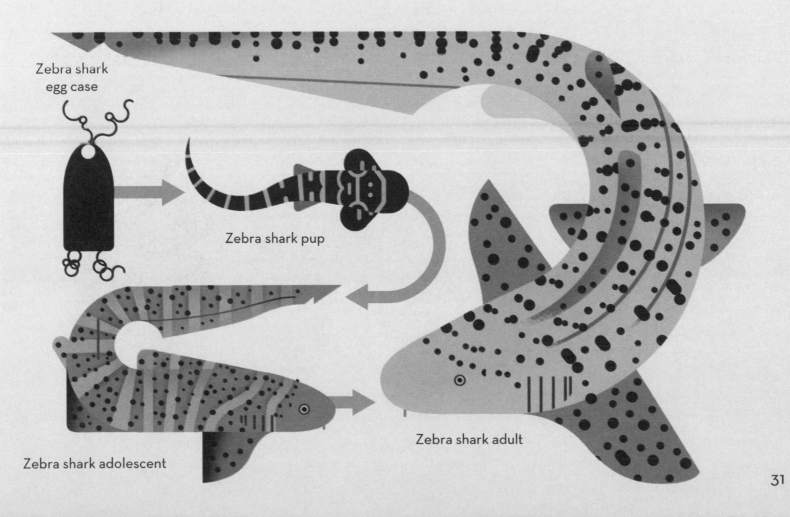

Zebra shark egg case

Zebra shark pup

Zebra shark adolescent

Zebra shark adult

SHARK MYTHOLOGY

Sharks have been prominent in human culture and mythology throughout our history. Many cultures greatly respect the shark, especially in places where many shark species are found in surrounding waters.

Shark Tooth Necklace

Legend has it that a young warrior dove into the sea to fight the lord of sharks and eventually emerged alone, wearing a tooth from the defeated shark around his neck. Today, many surfers and divers will wear a shark's tooth around their neck to provide protection from sharks when in the water.

Mäna

Some Yolngu aboriginal people of Australia believe they are descended from a divine shark called Mäna. While Mäna was sleeping on a beach, an ancestor from another clan speared him. In anger, Mäna chewed his way through the land, creating rivers in the process and leaving his teeth on the riverbanks. These teeth became Pandanus trees, which today have leaves similar to shark's teeth.

Interpretation of aboriginal art depicting Mäna

Ka-moho-ali'i

There are many shark gods in Hawaiian culture, but the chief of them is Ka-moho-ali'i. He could take on the form of any fish, and was known to guide Hawaiians home from sea if they offered him a drink known as **awa**.

Dakuwaqa

In Fijian folklore, Dakuwaqa is a half-man, half-shark god that protects fishermen while at sea. The legend has it that he once tried to conquer an island, but was confronted by an octopus goddess who grabbed Dakuwaqa with her many arms and squeezed him very tight. Defeated, Dakuwaqa begged for his life and promised to become the protector of the surrounding waters instead.

PLENTY MORE FISH IN THE SEA?

Shark populations are at serious risk and many species are now considered vulnerable. Some estimates suggest that humans may kill more than eleven thousand sharks an hour. The first shark to be put on the US endangered list was our old friend, the scalloped hammerhead shark.

Sharks are often caught as **bycatch**, which means they are picked up by accident in fishermen's nets or snagged on fishing hooks. But sharks are often hunted on purpose too: sometimes as a sport, or to be sold. Shark meat can be eaten, their skin can be used for leather, and their liver provides oil. In some parts of the world, sharks are caught purely for their fins to be used in soup.

These wonderful creatures are incredibly important to the ecosystems they live in. Nature is a delicate balancing act, and upsetting it can set off a chain reaction of harmful consequences.

Whitetip reef sharks
in a coral reef

What Can We Do?

One of the best ways you can help sharks is to keep their oceans healthy. Here are some things you can do to help:

1. Walking, biking, and being conscious about how much electricity and heating you use can help reduce your carbon footprint. Carbon is absorbed by the ocean, but too much of it will make the water too acidic for marine life.

2. If you own fish as pets, try to make sure they aren't wild caught fish, and don't release them into the ocean—they could mess with its fragile ecosystem.

3. Eating sustainable seafood helps make sure that your food has been caught in a way that won't negatively affect the ocean. Look for this symbol when food shopping.

CERTIFIED
SUSTAINABLE
SEAFOOD
MSC
www.msc.org

4. Plastic waste often ends up in the ocean and causes the deaths of thousands of marine animals every year. You can help by recycling, and always clean up after yourself when you've spent a day at the beach.

35

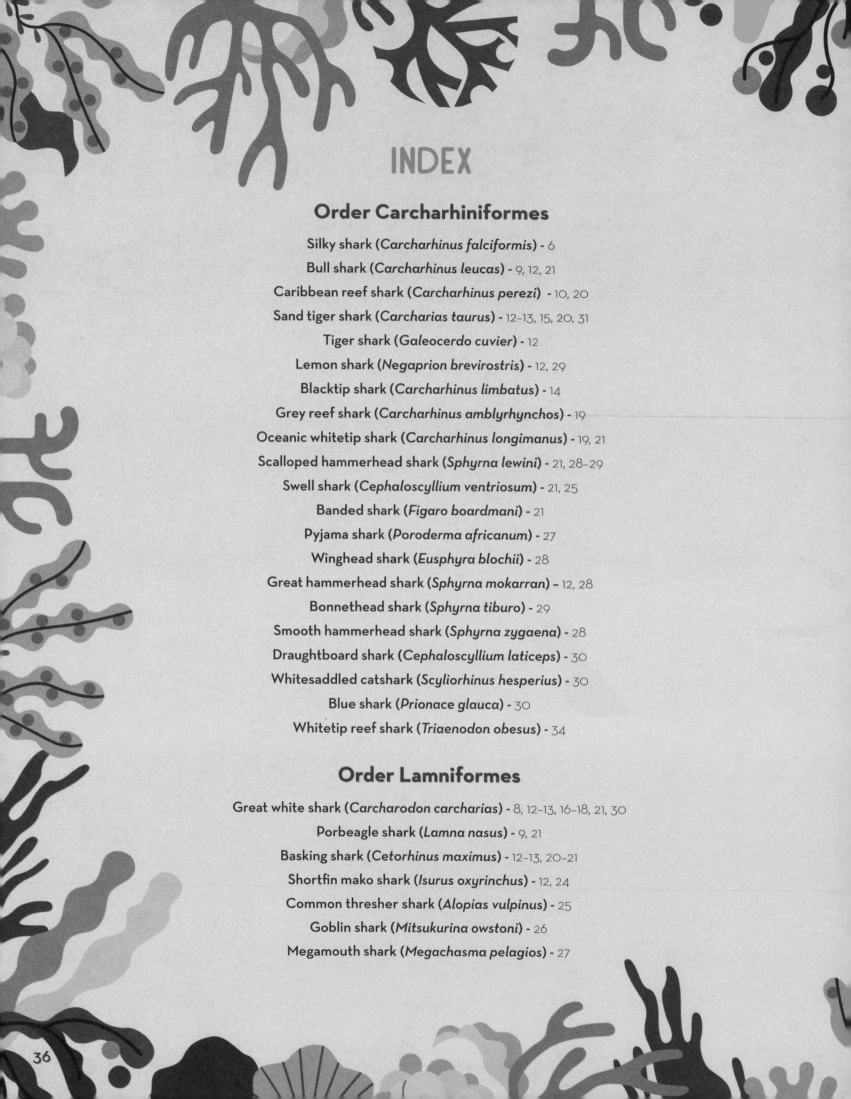

INDEX

Order Carcharhiniformes

Order Lamniformes

Order Orectolobiformes

Blind shark (*Brachaelurus waddi*) - 9, 20

Tawny nurse shark (*Nebrius ferrugineus*) - 10

Nurse shark (*Ginglymostoma cirratum*) - 25

Tasselled wobbegong shark (*Eucrossorhinus dasypogon*) - 15

Whale shark (*Rhincodon typus*) - 20-22

Epaulette shark (*Hemiscyllium ocellatum*) - 24

Zebra shark (*Stegostoma fasciatum*) - 31

Order Heterodontiformes

Japanese bullhead shark (*Heterodontus japonicus*) - 9, 21

Port Jackson shark (*Heterodontus portusjacksoni*) - 12-13

Horn shark (*Heterodontus francisci*) - 27, 30

Order Hexanchiformes

Broadnose sevengill shark (*Notorynchus cepedianus*) - 9, 12, 20

Frilled shark (*Chlamydoselachus anguineus*) - 12, 27

Order Squatiniformes

Sand devil shark (*Squatina dumeril*) - 9, 21

Ornate angel shark (*Squatina tergocellata*) - 26

Order Pristiophoriformes

Common sawshark (*Pristiophorus cirratus*) - 9, 20

Tropical sawshark (*Pristiophorus delicatus*) - 26

Order Squaliformes

Mandarin dogfish shark (*Cirrhigaleus barbifer*) - 9, 21

Cookiecutter shark (*Isistius brasiliensis*) - 12, 15, 20

Spurdog shark (*Squalus acanthias*) - 18, 20

Dwarf lanternshark (*Etmopterus fusus*) - 20, 23

Birdbeak dogfish shark (*Deania calcea*) - 26

If you like this, you'll love ...

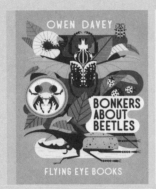
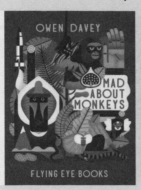

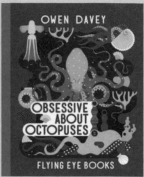

For Tom & Joe, my smart and wonderful brothers

First published in 2016 by Flying Eye Books, an imprint
of Nobrow Ltd. 27 Westgate Street, London, E8 3RL.
First American edition published 2021.

Text and illustrations © Owen Davey 2016.

Consultant: Dr Helen Scales

1 3 5 7 9 10 8 6 4 2

Published in the US by Nobrow (US) Inc.
Printed in Poland on FSC® certified paper.

ISBN: 978-1-83874-986-6
www.flyingeyebooks.com